On April 4, 1968, Dr. Martin Luther King, Jr., was assassinated while standing on the balcony outside his room at the Lorraine Motel in Memphis, Tennessee. This is the story of how that motel became the National Civil Rights Museum.

★ "Duncan's and Smith's informative, affecting collaboration is the next best thing to an actual trip to the museum."

—*Publishers Weekly,*
starred review

"Duncan's paean of praise to 'everyday people' makes it clear that it only takes courage, determination, and unity to make the world a better place."

—*School Library Journal*

"A vivid pictorial introduction . . . as well as detailed text . . . familiarize children with a turbulent time in the nation's history."

—*American Bookseller*

"The visual juxtaposition of past and present provides a moving context for the writing."

—*Booklist*

THE NATIONAL CIVIL RIGHTS MUSEUM

☆ CELEBRATES ☆

Everyday People

BY ALICE FAYE DUNCAN

PHOTOGRAPHS BY J. GERARD SMITH

Troll Medallion

In memory of Sister Thea Bowman—
                    A.F.D.

To Anne, for all her love and encouragement,
and
for all who dare to dream
I dedicate this book—
                    J.G.S.

Text copyright © 1995 by Alice Faye Duncan.

Photographs copyright © 1995 by J. Gerard Smith.

Additional credits and acknowledgments appear on page 64, which constitutes an extension of this copyright notice.

Published by Troll Medallion, an imprint and trademark of Troll Communications L.L.C.

First published in hardcover by BridgeWater Books.

Printed in the United States of America.

10 9 8 7 6 5 4 3 2 1

Library of Congress Cataloging-in-Publication Data

Duncan, Alice Faye.
The National Civil Rights Museum celebrates everyday people / Alice Faye Duncan; photos by J. Gerard Smith.
p.   cm.
ISBN 0-8167-3502-6 (lib.)   ISBN 0-8167-3503-4 (pbk.)
1. National Civil Rights Museum—Juvenile literature.   2. Afro-Americans—Civil rights—Juvenile literature.
3. Civil rights movements—United States—History—20th century—Juvenile literature.   4. United States—Race
relations—Juvenile literature.
I. Smith, J. Gerard   II. Title.
E185.615.D83   1995   326.1'196073'007476819—dc20   94-15831

FOREWORD

The National Civil Rights Museum Celebrates EVERYDAY PEOPLE explores the civil rights movement in America from 1954 to 1968, using select exhibits at the museum as a framework. The lives of some activists have been well documented here, while others may have been left unnoted. Limited space makes it impossible to address the contributions of everyone.

Nevertheless, this book is a tribute to the named and unnamed heroes and heroines who fought for equal rights in the United States of America. It is intended to remind us, page after page, that struggle precedes peace.

Top left and bottom: The entrance to the Lorraine Motel, now the National Civil Rights Museum. *Top right:* Michael Pavlovsky's *Movement to Overcome*, a statue in the entrance hall.

INTRODUCTION

In the city of Memphis, Tennessee, there is a most important motel. It stands downtown at the corner of Calhoun and Mulberry Streets, and everyone who comes through its doors is a welcome guest. Visitors, however, do not check into the motel with luggage, and they never stay overnight. The Lorraine Motel no longer serves as a lodging for weary travelers. Today it is a historic landmark. It is the unforgettable place where America's great dreamer and civil rights leader Dr. Martin Luther King, Jr., was murdered in the spring of 1968.

Even before the death of Dr. King, the motel at 450 Mulberry Street had an interesting history. Originally it was the Windsor Hotel when Walter and Loree Bailey purchased the L-shaped building in 1942. They renamed their new business the Lorraine. For over twenty years, it was one of only a few motels in Memphis where black Americans could get a room for the night. Some of the motel's celebrated clients included such entertainers as Aretha Franklin, B. B. King, and Nat King Cole, as well as baseball legend Jackie Robinson.

Often when Dr. King stopped in Memphis, he stayed at the Lorraine. During these visits, he preached strongly against the mistreatment of black Americans and other people of color. He spoke out against all forms of hatred and encouraged his listeners to protest, march, and boycott to win their rights. He encouraged them to ignore skin color and love all people.

Although the civil rights leader condemned violence and hatred, there were women and men who wanted Dr. King destroyed. They did not want him encouraging people to march and protest until all Americans were given full rights as citizens. They wanted the dreamer killed. And on April 4, 1968, it happened. Dr. King was shot on the second-floor balcony of the Lorraine Motel in Memphis.

Following the tragedy, the Lorraine Motel became a symbol of the civil rights struggle in the United States. Travelers from around the world would come to take pictures of the balcony where Dr. King was killed. Visitors would ask employees questions about that sad day in April. Then they would take home their snapshots and collected stories to share what they had seen.

The next years passed quickly as Dr. King's dream began to come true. Black Americans started to have better job opportunities. Black and white children found themselves going to schools of the same quality, playing at the same parks, and living in the same neighborhoods. Black people could exercise their right to vote, and life in America grew better. But for the Lorraine Motel, times grew worse as criminals, such as drug dealers, moved into the building. Dr. King's death place had become an eyesore—dirty, unkempt, and unsafe.

The balcony of the Lorraine Motel where Dr. King was killed.

Movement to Overcome inspires visitors by depicting courage and determination.

Many wondered what would happen to the Lorraine and asked themselves whether it should be saved. For Dr. King's widow, Coretta Scott King, the Lorraine was only a reminder of pain and heartache. She wanted the building torn down. But a group of businesspeople and lawyers in Memphis had a vision. They wanted to turn the old motel into a museum that would capture the sights, sounds, and tensions of the civil rights struggle. They wanted to make the motel a tribute to the common folk, the everyday people, who sang, marched, sat in, boycotted, and went to jail until all Americans were given equal rights under the law. This group called itself the Lorraine Foundation. And in 1982, the members bought the run-down motel in order to make their vision come alive.

Getting state funds and contributions from local businesses to pay for the museum project took a great deal of effort. But the foundation did not give up on its vision and searched until support was found. For three years, the motel remained closed while planning and renovations took place. Then, on August 31, 1991, the great moment arrived. The Lorraine was opened as the country's National Civil Rights Museum.

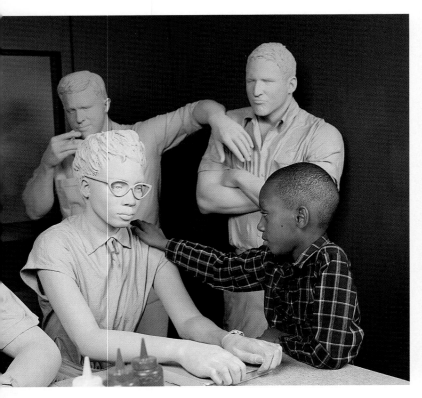

Visitors stand before the Sit-in exhibit and a replica of a Birmingham jail cell.

Visitors discover that the main exhibits in the museum capture the sounds, actions, and feelings of the period between 1954 and 1968. The exhibits are interactive, allowing guests to sit, touch, and listen. Thus, the Montgomery Bus Boycott exhibit permits you to hop on a bus and stand by a tired Rosa Parks, who fought for her rights by refusing to give up her seat to a white bus rider. Guests at the Student Sit-in exhibit hop onto a stool at a restored department-store lunch counter to view how college students were abused when they quietly protested for their right to be served in a public place. At the Freedom Riders exhibit, visitors can touch the outside of a badly burned Greyhound bus. The bus resembles those used in the dangerous 1961 Freedom Rides where people rode to protest segregated bus terminals.

During a tour of the National Civil Rights Museum, visitors can march with life-size protesters demanding voting rights, fair housing, and equal pay. They can stand before the Little Rock exhibit to view angry whites attempting to scare black students away from Central High School. Visitors can also feel what it is like to be in an Alabama jail cell like the one used to hold men, women, and children who marched for freedom in the city of Birmingham.

As the tour of the National Civil Rights Museum comes to an end, visitors walk through the Lorraine Motel until they reach the last exhibit—Rooms 306 and 307. Dr. Martin Luther King, Jr., was standing in front of Room 306 at the instant when he was shot. Room 307 was the room he occupied during his last stay at the motel. While visitors stand between these two rooms, they can read about the great leader's life and feel the power of the moment. In the background, gospel singer Mahalia Jackson croons her tender version of "Precious Lord," a slow and sorrowful tune that is often sung at funerals.

As Mahalia Jackson sings, visitors remember all that they have felt and seen during their tour of the National Civil Rights Museum. And suddenly everything comes together. We begin to understand that the civil rights movement in the United States was a struggle fought by everyday people like you and me. They were not rich, famous, or exceptional—just bold and determined to fight for freedom. The National Civil Rights Museum at the Lorraine Motel recreates their struggle, and we are left to carry the torch.

The museum provides newspapers from the movement and an opportunity to walk amid statues of marchers.

All aboard! Do you hear the engine roaring? Did people say that they were ready to ride? Then let's take a tour of the National Civil Rights Museum at the Lorraine Motel.

On this excursion, we will discover everyday people and learn about their efforts to fight against segregation and racial inequalities. They are heroes and heroines, though many of their names are unknown. History books do not tell who every one of them is. But because they stood for justice, the United States of America is a better place for all of us.

Today people of all races in America claim freedom. Blacks no longer have to enter through the back door of white-owned establishments. They no longer must drink from public water fountains with signs that read FOR COLORED ONLY. Because thousands of everyday people refused to remain second-class citizens, the races are no longer separate. Today we go to school together. We pray in the same houses of worship. Today we play on the same sports teams. We laugh. We talk. We go to the same parties. And friends are not turned away from our homes because they are a certain color.

Life in America has not always been this accepting. Before there was unity, there was strife. Before there was unity, there was struggle. A powerful movement had to happen. It was a movement conducted by ordinary men and women with everyday lives. No royalty. No riches. No fame. As we tour the National Civil Rights Museum, we will learn about their unyielding courage.

Young people have fun on a bus like the one that Rosa Parks rode.

The first stop is the deep South: states such as Alabama, Georgia, Louisiana, Arkansas. During the 1950s, these and other southern states were known for their separation of the races. White and black people did not mingle with one another. This was called *segregation,* and it was the law in these states. For example, black home owners could buy houses only in all-black neighborhoods. Black students could go only to all-black schools, even if another school was closer. In restaurants, black citizens were seated in the rear beside the restaurant's kitchen. In public places like department stores, black shoppers could not use a rest room unless the sign on the door was marked COLORED.

Public transportation was a problem as well. When black riders boarded a bus, by law they had to take the farthest seat in the back. And if these riders found themselves sitting in the front, they were expected to give their seat away to any white person standing.

Students have been known to vandalize the statue of the bus driver who shouted at Rosa Parks.

Young visitor whispers her thanks to a statue of Rosa Parks.

In the 1950s, public transportation was the cheapest way to get around town. Black Americans rode the buses daily. For a small fee, local transportation would take them all across the city. But the emotional price they had to pay was no small matter. Bus drivers were permitted to speak to adult black riders as if they were children. "Get up, girl!" they would shout. "Get up, boy!" And at that moment, black bus riders were supposed to stand and give away their seats.

In the fall of 1955, a proud woman named Rosa Parks had seen and suffered as much humiliation as she was willing to take. She was an everyday person, just like you. Her husband was a barber. She worked as a seamstress, and she was tired. She was tired of cruel bus drivers and segregation laws that did not make sense. So Mrs. Parks decided that something had to change.

She demanded justice, and the Montgomery Bus Boycott exhibit celebrates her bravery. Visitors bear witness as a life-size statue of a bus driver shouts out orders to the seated statue of a weary Rosa Parks, who refuses to take her "proper place" at the back of the bus.

The date was December 1, 1955. The place was Montgomery, Alabama— a southern town where Rosa Parks worked in a department store. After work that day, Mrs. Parks boarded a city bus to ride home. There was a seat available in the middle of the bus, and she sat in it. As other riders boarded, the white bus driver ordered Mrs. Parks to give her seat to a white man who was standing. She ignored the driver and kept her seat. Her rage had reached its limit. And because she stood up for her rights, the bus driver had her arrested.

At the police station, she had her fingerprints taken like a criminal. On December 5, she was convicted and fined ten dollars plus court fees. When details of the arrest became public, a group of black women—the Women's Political Council—took action. They asked ministers and civic leaders to help organize a boycott against the Montgomery City Lines bus company. One of the ministers to answer their call was twenty-six-year-old Dr. Martin Luther King, Jr.

Under the leadership of Dr. King, the black citizens of Montgomery held their bus boycott from December 5, 1955 to December 20, 1956. For over a year, black men, women, and children did not ride city buses. Instead, they formed car pools with neighbors or fellow church members. They rode in taxis that charged less than regular rates. And if they could not form a car pool or take a taxi, they walked.

Through the boycott, black citizens demanded courteous treatment by bus operators. They wanted to be seated on a first-come, first-served basis. They also demanded that blacks be allowed to apply for jobs as bus drivers. Dr. King presented these demands to city leaders, who did not take any action. And so the case was taken to the highest court in the United States.

The Supreme Court examined the Montgomery case and ruled that segregation on Alabama buses was unconstitutional. So, in December of 1956, Dr. King, Rosa Parks, and other black citizens of Montgomery paid their fares and rode the city buses once again. And this time, they sat wherever they pleased!

Top: **Rosa Parks rides the city bus after the Supreme Court decision.**
Bottom: **Rosa Parks is fingerprinted in a Montgomery jail for refusing to give up her seat.**

Our next stop is the Little Rock exhibit. The year was 1957. Although the Supreme Court had ruled that black and white children should go to the same public schools, they were still not doing so.

In Little Rock, nine teenagers were to be the first black students to attend all-white Central High School. Their attendance meant that the school would be integrated, with blacks and whites part of the same student body. To discourage the black students from entering the building, Governor Orval Faubus posted members of the Arkansas National Guard outside the school. Taking their cue from the governor, mobs of angry white citizens hurled insults and threats at the students.

To stop the unruly mobs from disrupting procedures to integrate Central High, President Dwight D. Eisenhower sent federal troops to escort the nine black students inside the school. Thus, Eisenhower became the first president in the post–Civil War era to use armed soldiers to support the rights of black Americans.

Students in front of the statue of Governor Faubus take notes on the Little Rock exhibit.

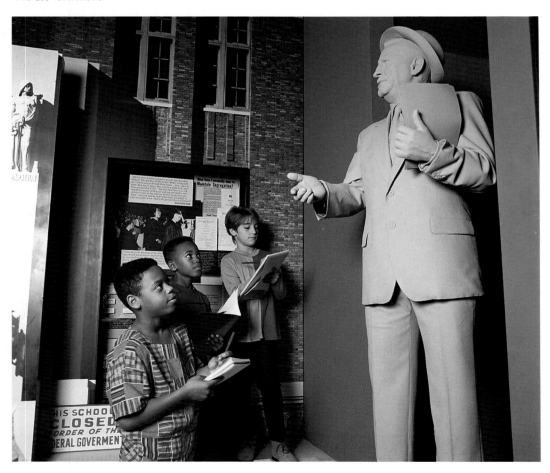

Visitors watch original Little Rock Nine news footage.

The black students assigned to Central High came to be known as the Little Rock Nine. They were Minniejean Brown, Elizabeth Eckford, Ernest Green, Thelma Mothershed, Melba Pattillo, Gloria Ray, Terrance Roberts, Jefferson Thomas, and Carlotta Walls.

On the September day that the Little Rock Nine were to enter Central High, Elizabeth Eckford did not get the message that she was to ride to school with the others. Instead, this brave girl faced a shouting white mob alone. According to witnesses, the mob was on its way to attack Elizabeth when a white woman quickly led her to safety.

Even after the federal troops arrived in Little Rock to escort the students onto their new campus, things did not calm down. The Little Rock Nine were still harassed by students and parents. Minniejean Brown was moved to pour chili on a white boy who called her vulgar names. Brown was suspended. Several weeks later, she was expelled from the school because she exchanged insults with a white girl.

White students shout insults as Elizabeth Eckford enters Central High School.

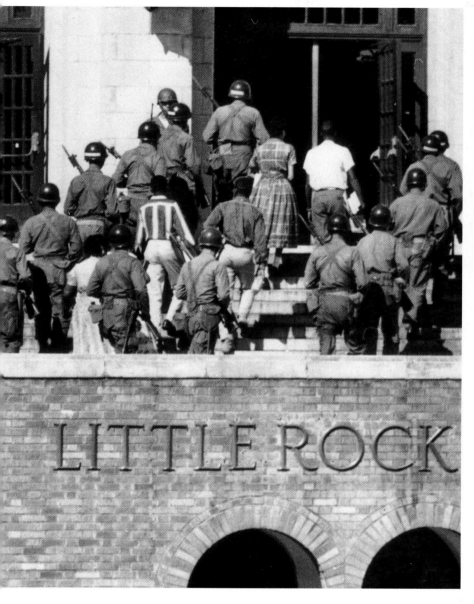

Left: Federal troops escort black students to class.
Right: Ernest Green graduates from Central High.

Of the nine students, Ernest Green was the only one to graduate from Central High School. "After I got that diploma," he said, "that was it. I had accomplished what I had come there for."

Just like you, Ernest Green and the Little Rock Nine were everyday people with dreams and ambitions. Like you, they wanted to learn. They wanted an equal opportunity to attend a decent school with up-to-date books and facilities. They integrated Central High and became living proof of the constitutional right of all Americans— no matter what the color of their skin—to a quality education.

After the Little Rock conflict, young people in America grew restless for change. In particular, college students were ready to make freedom a reality for all men, women, and children in the nation. To do this, they were prepared to fight and risk their lives. Their weapons of choice, however, were not fists or guns. In the 1960s, these young people chose to bring about change through nonviolent protests. Like Dr. Martin Luther King, Jr., and the black citizens of Montgomery, young people led boycotts. The student "sit-ins," as they were called, became one of the most popular and most effective forms of nonviolent protest in the '60s.

To conduct a sit-in, the students first identified stores that did not serve black customers at their lunch counters. Then they would take seats at these counters and ask to order. Black students were denied service because of segregation. When this happened, the students immediately informed the waiter and manager of the store that they would not move from their seats until fair treatment was given to black customers.

Students did not laugh or talk to one another during these protests. And when white customers came along to pour salt, ashes, and food on their heads, the students did not become violent. They simply took the abuse and remained in their seats, day after day.

The protesting students came so often and stayed so long that the segregated lunch counters suffered financially. The sit-ins were, therefore, effective. And they proved an important point: Young people had the power to change things.

Visitors sit at a lunch counter like the one where student protests began.

The National Civil Rights Museum documents the one student sit-in that began a wave of nonviolent protests all over the nation. This great sit-in took place in Greensboro, North Carolina, at the lunch counter of a Woolworth store.

Black students from North Carolina Agricultural and Technical College in Greensboro started the protest because they were upset over segregation and the mistreatment of black Americans. When the students began on February 1, 1960, they were determined to sit at the counter daily until the business changed its policies and served black customers with the same respect that it served whites.

Whites pour sugar, salt, and mustard over the heads of lunch counter demonstrators.

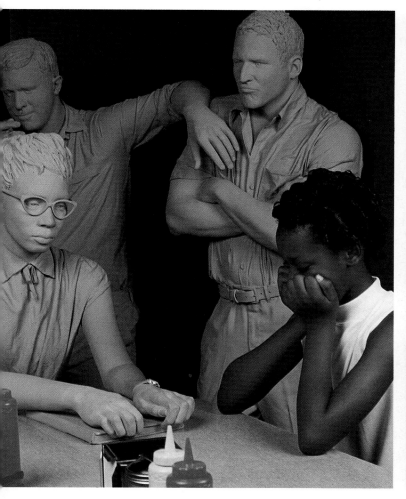

The Sit-in exhibit evokes feelings of struggle and strife.

During the first days of the sit-in, only black students participated. But by February 5, 1960, hundreds of black and white students sat together. According to their code, they were to enter the Woolworth neatly dressed. They were friendly at all times, though they were not treated in kind. Hecklers would often harass them, yet the harassment did not cause the protesters to give up their fight. They held on to the dream. They sat in day after day, and by July 1960, stores all over Greensboro were serving black and white customers at their lunch counters.

Following the Greensboro sit-ins, students extended their protests beyond lunch counters to restaurants, hotels, parks, swimming pools, and jobs. Student protests stretched across the country. From New York to Nashville, these college students were ordinary people who wanted to make a difference. So they did.

After the successful integration of lunch counters, young people moved on to desegregate interstate bus terminals. This was accomplished through what are remembered as the 1961 Freedom Rides.

The Congress of Racial Equality (CORE) and the Student Nonviolent Coordinating Committee (SNCC) were the two groups responsible for organizing students for the Freedom Rides that began in May 1961. During the dangerous trips, black and white members would board buses to travel together throughout the South. Their unity was the key to destroying segregation and unlawful practices directed against black travelers. These students had a clear purpose: They rode for freedom.

Left: **A bruised Freedom Rider.**
Right: **Freedom Riders nap in a Birmingham bus terminal.**

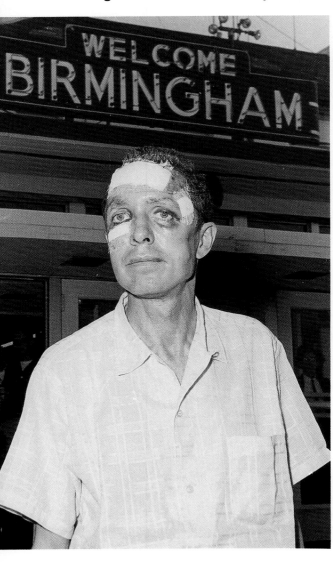

Passenger points to a segregation sign that is about to be torn down.

While on their journey, the Freedom Riders encountered stark violence and often came close to losing their lives. Angry mobs would identify their buses and flatten all the tires or set fire to the buses. These mobs also boarded the buses with planks and chains to beat the riders. Sometimes the traveling protesters were left sitting for days in cold bus terminals because bus drivers refused to drive them.

The Freedom Rides continued throughout the summer of 1961. The determined students would not let their will be broken. Though the government tried to convince them to stop riding—the trips were becoming more and more dangerous—the members of CORE and SNCC rode on! Then, in September of that same year, their efforts paid off: The Interstate Commerce Commission ended segregation in interstate bus terminals.

At the National Civil Rights Museum, visitors can stand before a Greyhound bus similar to the one that was burned outside of Anniston, Alabama, during the 1961 Freedom Rides. Visitors can see the charred, twisted metal and the gutted windows. It is a sight of terror, meant to remind people that hundreds of college students risked their lives so that all Americans can now travel in comfort.

Like you, the young Freedom Riders came from all over the nation. Some came from New York, Tennessee, Massachusetts, and Kansas. Others came from Illinois, Alabama, Georgia, Texas, and Washington, D. C. They were all colors and all religions. They suffered together. They committed themselves to the civil rights struggle when the United States government begged them to quit.

But the students did not quit. Together, they rode on to victory.

A badly burned Greyhound bus resembles the one destroyed in Anniston, Alabama.

The next stop is Birmingham, Alabama. The year was 1963. Dr. Martin Luther King, Jr., and a group of black ministers who worked together in the Southern Christian Leadership Conference (SCLC) were busy planning a huge list of nonviolent activities in the city. The ministers titled their big event Project "C," for "confrontation."

Project "C" was an attempt to desegregate public facilities and increase employment of black Americans in commerce and industry. To accomplish these goals, Dr. King and the SCLC planned mass marches, sit-ins, and boycotts of downtown businesses.

At the time, Theophilus Eugene "Bull" Connor was the public safety commissioner of Birmingham. He requested that the courts order Dr. King and his followers not to march in the city. Connor let them know that if they did, they would go to jail. Dr. King and his followers ignored this order and marched. And as Bull Connor had promised, they were arrested quickly.

On May 2, Dr. King and his followers marched again to protest segregation and limited employment opportunities for black citizens. Close to one thousand protesters supported Dr. King on this march. And again they, too, were arrested. Hundreds of youths went to jail.

The following day saw more protests. Close to two thousand people marched. Adults came with their children; college students came with their friends. It was a protest group of all ages.

As the marchers turned a corner, Public Safety Commissioner Connor ordered them to turn around. They refused and kept marching. Then an awful thing happened. Connor ordered firefighters to spray the protesters with big fire hoses powerful enough to rip bark from a tree. The high-pressure hoses pushed people's bodies against buildings and cars. To create more confusion and injury, police dogs were ordered to attack innocent marchers. As people fought for their lives, the rest of the nation witnessed their terror on the evening news and on the front pages of newspapers.

Top: **Attack dogs and fire hoses were just two tactics used to stop marchers in Birmingham.**
Bottom: **Visitors come to know the fear of protesters during the Project "C" demonstrations.**

Dr. Martin Luther King, Jr., peers between the bars of his jail cell.

After Dr. King's first arrest during Project "C" in Birmingham, some white ministers in the city made public statements that criticized the civil rights movement and its leader. The ministers called Dr. King and his followers "impatient." They called the marching "unwise and untimely." And they suggested that Dr. King and his followers should not fight for freedom, but wait for the local and federal governments to solve their problems.

Dr. King read about the ministers' statements while in jail. Immediately he was moved to write a response. He had to let them know why black citizens could not be silent and wait for the government—politicians had been slow to bring about change. So from his cell, with a single lightbulb hanging overhead, Dr. King wrote a letter that explained his followers' position and feelings.

I guess it is easy for those who have never felt the stinging darts of segregation to say, "Wait." But when you have seen vicious mobs lynch your mothers and fathers at will and drown your sisters and brothers at whim; when you have seen hate-filled policemen curse, kick, brutalize, and even kill your black brothers and sisters . . . then you will understand why we [black Americans] find it difficult to wait. There comes a time when the cup of endurance runs over, and men are no longer willing to be plunged into an abyss of injustice.

Because jail did not offer the luxury of adequate light and a typewriter, Dr. King wrote his letter in tiny handwriting on scraps of paper. His lawyer, Arthur Shores, then secretly carried it out of jail in a worn brown briefcase. With the passing of time, Dr. King's "Letter from a Birmingham Jail" has become a classic example of protest literature.

A youngster gets acquainted with the kind of place where Dr. King wrote his famous letter.

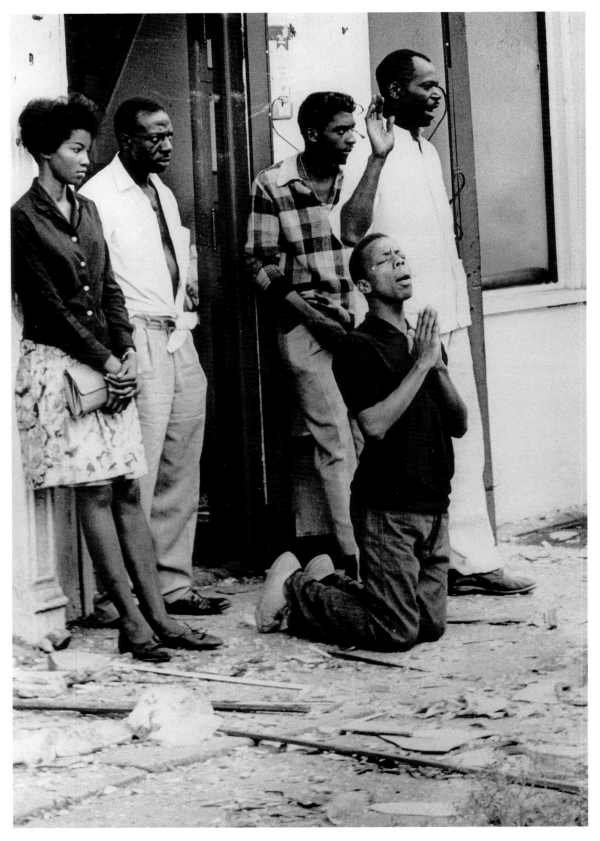

A young man kneels on a glass-littered sidewalk across the street from the ruins of the 16th Street Baptist Church.

A woman is rushed from the scene as a fire burns furiously in an all-black section of Birmingham, Alabama.

Dr. King and his followers continued to march in Birmingham. They continued to sit in, and they continued the boycott of businesses that did not treat black customers fairly. The protesters would not stop. Eventually business owners—desperate because they were losing customers and not making enough money to pay their bills—asked politicians to reach an agreement with Dr. King and his followers.

Under the agreements that were made, black Birmingham citizens were guaranteed desegregated lunch counters, rest rooms, sitting rooms, and drinking fountains in downtown department stores. They were also promised the development of a fair employment committee, along with the release of all the protesters who were still in jail.

When the white citizens of Birmingham heard about the agreements, many were happy for what the protesters had achieved. Others were upset. Several groups of angry whites showed their feelings by bombing houses, churches, cars, and businesses that belonged to blacks. This senseless violence prompted President John F. Kennedy to set the wheels in motion for what was to become the Civil Rights Act of 1964.

Youngsters sing songs of freedom, march for their rights, and go to jail.

At the National Civil Rights Museum, the Birmingham exhibit highlights the contributions of those adults and children who fought for change in Alabama. The exhibit documents their struggle and reveals that children in the city fought just as hard as the adults. These children were just like you. They were students with homework to do and tests to take. They were brave, they were bold, and they marched. They attended church meetings with Dr. King. They participated in sit-ins and in boycotts. They made a contribution to the movement, and, thanks to their efforts, Birmingham changed.

Like the adults who marched, the children in the movement also had to pay a price for their boldness and effort. They, too, were put in cold, crowded jail cells, and many of them were suspended from school because of their participation.

Students crowd into a holding cell like the ones where young protesters were kept.

Following the Birmingham experience, civil rights leaders banded together to plan a march on Washington, D. C., the nation's capital. The march had several purposes: It would demand that the government ensure voting rights for black citizens and equal access to decent housing, jobs, public accommodations, and top-quality schools. The march would be an attempt to gain economic and political freedom for all black citizens and to gain human rights for all of the nation's people who suffered from poverty and the lack of opportunity.

The March on Washington was held on Wednesday, August 28, 1963. People from around the country came to the Lincoln Memorial to participate in the event—black people, white people, young and old. Some had come by bus, some by train or plane. Others had traveled by car, while some had walked from their cities to the nation's capital. In all, over 250,000 protesters marched on Washington.

The weather was pleasant that day as several civil rights leaders delivered speeches and famous singers celebrated the moment with song. Finally Dr. Martin Luther King, Jr., was introduced.

When Dr. King moved to the microphone, the 250,000 protesters cheered with excitement. They applauded the great leader. They waved their protest signs high. Then Dr. King delivered to the nation his remarkable "I Have a Dream" speech, which continues to promote unity among the races.

> *So I say to you, my friends, that even though we must face the difficulties of today and tomorrow, I still have a dream. It is a dream deeply rooted in the American dream that one day this nation will rise up and live out the true meaning of its creed. . . . I have a dream that one day, every valley shall be exalted, every hill and mountain shall be made low, the rough places shall be made plain, and the crooked places shall be made straight . . . and all flesh shall see it together.*

An aerial view of the Lincoln Memorial, where 250,000 protesters marched for their rights on August 28, 1963.

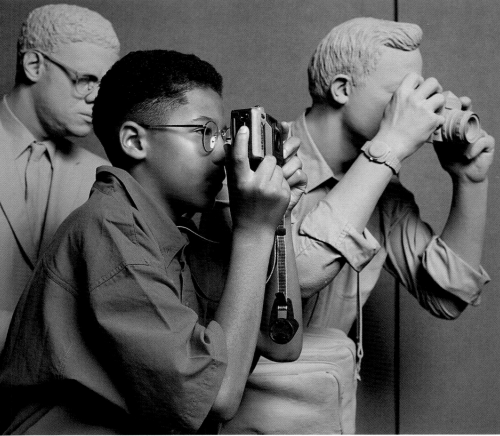

Young boy mounts podium, while others stand amid statues of photojournalists at the exhibit.

The March on Washington was so large and included so many people from different walks of life that photographers for newspapers and magazines were sent to Washington to take pictures. All the major television networks sent reporters and camera crews to report stories. Thus, people across the nation were able to witness the power of that day in print and on television.

Dr. King delivers his stirring "I Have a Dream" speech.

Top: Students display their own protest signs at the March on Washington exhibit.
Bottom: Leaders of the March on Washington lock arms as thousands protest for their rights.

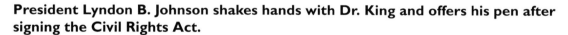

When people think about the March on Washington, they recall the protesters and a sea of waving signs. There were thousands and thousands of signs. Some were homemade; some were printed. Some were big; some were small. Yet they all had one thing in common. Each sign made a demand for justice. They contained messages, such as WE DEMAND DECENT HOUSING! WE DEMAND JOBS NOW! WE DEMAND AN END TO POLICE BRUTALITY! WE DEMAND VOTING RIGHTS!

All of these issues were important to protesters because black Americans did not enjoy the comfortable lifestyle that many white Americans enjoyed. In the workplace, black Americans were paid less money than white Americans. In the world of politics, many black Americans were kept from voting. And in housing, black Americans were often forced to live in slums even when they had the money to move to a better place.

Marchers carried their signs to Washington to bring equality to all people. One year later, they came to see the positive results of their labor. President Lyndon B. Johnson signed the Civil Rights Act of 1964. This act outlawed discrimination on the job. It outlawed discrimination in public places. It ordered the desegregation of schools and outlawed discrimination on the basis of sex.

With the passing of this new act, however, there was no room to rest easy. Other changes were in store. So the protesters gathered their signs and moved on to continue their fight for justice.

President Lyndon B. Johnson shakes hands with Dr. King and offers his pen after signing the Civil Rights Act.

Several boys walk across replica of the Edmund Pettus Bridge while keeping an eye on looming statues of state troopers.

The next exhibit at the National Civil Rights Museum documents the march from Selma to Montgomery in Alabama. This event began on March 7, 1965. It was a Sunday, windy and cool. Over five hundred men, women, and children prepared for another protest. They would walk from Selma to the state capital, where they were to tell Governor George Wallace that it was time for black citizens to receive full voting rights in Alabama. Montgomery was about fifty miles away from Selma, so protesters carried bedrolls and bags of food on their backs. They prepared themselves for a long journey as they proceeded out of Brown's Chapel Methodist Church.

Governor Wallace warned protesters not to march. He told them that they would be stopped, but they marched on, anyway. They marched to gain voting rights for black citizens in Alabama.

When the hundreds of marchers reached the Edmund Pettus Bridge in East Selma, which led the way to Montgomery, they were met by a terrible surprise. On the other side of the bridge, state troopers with nightsticks, whips, and gas masks were waiting to stop the march. Protesters, however, kept marching. Like the protesters in Selma, museum guests can walk over a replica of the Edmund Pettus Bridge, the beginning of the journey to Alabama's state capital.

Major John Cloud asked the protesters to return to Brown's Chapel for their safety. He asked them to go home, but no one turned back. So Major Cloud ordered his men to advance. Immediately the troopers rushed into the protesters and began an attack with their nightsticks and fists. Children began to cry. Adults began to scream, and in the middle of all the drama, protesters were bombed with tear gas. The tear gas was so thick that it covered the street like a dense blanket of fog.

This day in American history came to be known as "Bloody Sunday." It is significant because, after President Johnson witnessed the protesters and their suffering, he committed himself to ending all practices that denied people their right to vote. On August 6, President Johnson signed the Voting Rights Act of 1965. This act ensured that all black citizens, all poor citizens, and all non-English-speaking citizens could exercise their right to vote in local and national elections. A brand-new day was on the horizon.

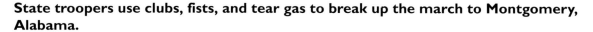

State troopers use clubs, fists, and tear gas to break up the march to Montgomery, Alabama.

National Guardsmen use bayonets to block Beale Street in Memphis as protesters march.

Following the Voting Rights Act of 1965, black Americans throughout the South registered to vote. Then they went to exercise their new voting power, electing black politicians to several local and national offices. This proved that the United States was clearly taking steps toward justice and equality. However, the stubborn city of Memphis, Tennessee, still tried its hardest not to change. The National Civil Rights Museum documents this historical period.

The year was 1968, and black sanitation workers in Memphis were on strike because white city leaders refused to recognize their union and their demands for an increase in pay. The museum exhibit reveals that these strikers wore big, boldly printed signs that read I AM A MAN, to show that they were proud and would not settle for injustice. To help the workers obtain better wages, Dr. Martin Luther King, Jr., came to Memphis and organized a protest march. The march was not successful because it was interrupted by looting and rioting.

During the first protest, Dr. King did not accomplish anything for the striking workers, but he was determined to help their cause. So he returned to Memphis and stayed at the Lorraine Motel, where he prepared for a second march. After all, these men were hard workers. Their jobs were important to the entire city, and they deserved better wages.

Memphis sanitation workers were determined to win better wages through nonviolent protests.

When Dr. King returned to Memphis on April 3, he checked into Room 307 at the Lorraine Motel and met with several black sanitation workers, reporters, and several staff members from the SCLC who were helping to coordinate the march. Later, during the evening, he went to Mason Temple to speak with the people who would participate in the march. Dr. King encouraged them to conduct a peaceful protest, and to walk in the spirit of love and nonviolence. He also asked that they not grow weary or give up on their efforts, for America was changing, and justice would be achieved just as he dreamed. He asked the audience to do whatever was necessary to help the movement.

> *Let us develop a kind of dangerous unselfishness. Let us rise up tonight with a greater readiness. Let us stand with a greater determination. And let us move on in these powerful days, these days of challenge to make America what it ought to be.*

While on the journey for freedom, Dr. King received numerous death threats. To prepare his followers, family, and friends for the possibility of his passing, Dr. King told them all about the death threats and said that they did not scare him—he was willing to sacrifice his life for the movement. He was ready and willing to die for freedom.

The National Civil Rights Museum at the Lorraine Motel stands in downtown Memphis, Tennessee.

After his speech at Mason Temple, Dr. King never led another march. He never preached another sermon or spoke to another band of followers, because on April 4, 1968, he was assassinated. The nation's great dreamer was shot by a sniper's bullet while standing on the balcony of the Lorraine Motel. The time was 6 P.M., and, in that instant, many Americans feel that the greatest chapter in the civil rights movement died with the passing of Dr. King and his courageous spirit.

Although Dr. King had discussed his own death, this did not remove the shock of his assassination outside Room 306. The brutal murder shook the world. It left millions of people heartbroken. His friends the Reverends Ralph Abernathy, Jesse Jackson, Andrew Young, and Billy Kyles were especially shaken because they were at the motel when Dr. King was murdered.

He had been their great teacher. He had taught them how to organize protests. He had taught them how to win a fight for justice without the use of foul language, fists, or guns. Dr. King had taught them how to bring about change through love, and, like the rest of the world, they would miss him deeply.

**Dr. Martin Luther King, Jr., on the balcony where, one day later, he would be slain.
With him are Hosea Williams, Jesse Jackson, and Ralph Abernathy.**

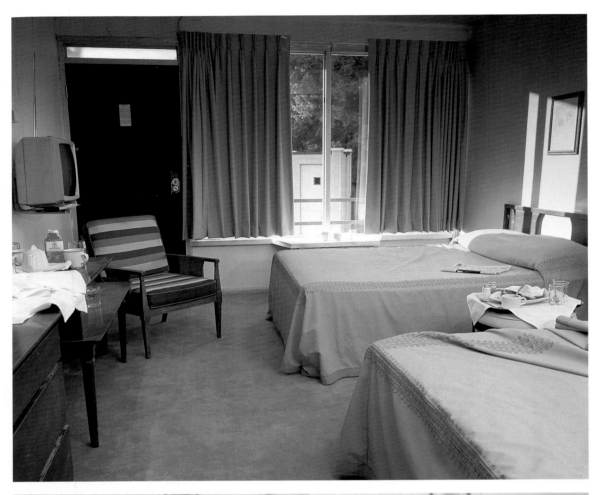

Dr. King was killed in front of Room 306, which has been made to look just as it did on the day of his death.

The last exhibit at the National Civil Rights Museum brings us inside the Lorraine Motel. The Lorraine's Rooms 306 and 307 are just as they were on the day of Dr. King's final visit. The curtains are open. There are empty coffee cups, drinking glasses, and used ashtrays sitting on the furniture. Between two beds in Room 307, visitors also see the last dinner that Dr. King shared with the Reverend Ralph Abernathy.

Outside Room 306, there is a white wreath that hangs on the balcony. People from all over the world come to see it. They take pictures of the wreath or sometimes they just stand before it and cry, for the wreath marks the very spot where America's great dreamer lost his life in the struggle for justice and equality.

When young people reach the last exhibit at the Lorraine Motel, they often ask, "Is the civil rights movement over now?" The answer is no. Our struggle continues because today we must work to end social problems like poverty and homelessness. We must work to stop police brutality and gang violence. We must fight to end racial prejudice, physical abuse, and all other forms of hatred.

Like the thousands of everyday people who walked with Dr. King, we must stand together in the spirit of unity. We must look around our world and try to correct the many wrongs that we see. Our road will not be easy, but we can do it. Like Rosa Parks, we can do it. Like the Little Rock Nine, we can do it. Like the Freedom Riders and the people of Selma, we can do it. Together we can make a difference. Then tomorrow's people will look upon our efforts and be inspired to do the same.

Youngsters stand together before *Movement to Overcome* and reflect on their visit to the museum.

The balcony then . . . and now.

CHRONOLOGY

1954 The Supreme Court declares that segregation in public schools is unconstitutional.

1955 Rosa Parks refuses to surrender her seat on the bus to a white rider and is arrested. Her protest inspires the Montgomery bus boycott.

1956 The Supreme Court rules segregation on Alabama buses unconstitutional.

1957 Dr. Martin Luther King, Jr., Bayard Rustin, and Stanley Levison form the Southern Christian Leadership Conference (SCLC) to achieve equality for black Americans through nonviolent protests.

1957 The Little Rock Nine integrate Central High School in Little Rock, Arkansas.

1960 Sit-ins in Greensboro, North Carolina, inspire students throughout the South to protest and boycott businesses that do not serve black Americans.

1961 CORE and SNCC begin freedom rides that lead to desegregation of interstate bus stations.

1961 Malcolm X founds *Muhamad Speaks*, the official publication of the Nation of Islam.

1963 Dr. Martin Luther King, Jr., is arrested during Project "C" demonstrations and writes his "Letter from a Birmingham Jail" to explain why black Americans must protest.

1963 Bayard Rustin and A. Philip Randolph, along with other civil rights leaders, organize the March on Washington to express the economic and political concerns of minorities.

1964   President Lyndon B. Johnson signs the Civil Rights Act, a milestone in the struggle for equality.

1964   Dr. Martin Luther King, Jr., is awarded the Nobel Peace Prize.

1964   Malcolm X leaves the Nation of Islam and becomes a leading spokesperson on racial pride. Founds the Organization of African-American Unity.

1965   Malcolm X is assassinated on February 21, 1965.

1965   State troopers attack protesters on the Edmund Pettus Bridge. Dr. Martin Luther King, Jr., and the Reverend Ralph Abernathy plan a march in Alabama from Selma to Montgomery to demand voting rights for black Alabama citizens.

1965   President Johnson signs the Voting Rights Act, ensuring that all black citizens could exercise their right to vote in local and national elections.

1967   SNCC becomes a militant group under the leadership of H. Rap Brown.

1968   Dr. Martin Luther King, Jr., arrives in Memphis, Tennessee, to organize a protest march of black sanitation workers. He delivers his final sermon at Mason Temple.

1968   Dr. Martin Luther King, Jr., is assassinated at the Lorraine Motel in Memphis, Tennessee. *In 1969 James Earl Ray was sentenced to ninety-nine years in jail for the murder of Dr. King.*

SUGGESTED FURTHER READING

Adams, Russell L. *Great Negroes Past and Present.* Chicago: Afro-Am Publishing Co., 1984. An encyclopedia of heroic and influential Africans and African Americans who have made various contributions to the world. (Ages 10-up)

Greene, Carol. *Thurgood Marshall: First African-American Supreme Court Justice.* Chicago: Children's Press, 1991. Biography of the first African American appointed to the Supreme Court. (Ages 5–9)

Haskins, James. *Outward Dreams: Black Inventors and Their Inventions.* New York: Bantam Books, 1992. Photographs and biographies of African-American men and women who changed the world with their inventions. (Ages 10-up)

Levine, Ellen. *Freedom's Children.* New York: Putnam, 1993. Photographs and narratives from children of the civil rights movement. (Ages 11-up)

———. *If You Lived at the Time of Martin Luther King.* New York: Scholastic, 1990. A general account of organizations and leaders that made the civil rights movement what it was. (Ages 7–12)

Myers, Walter Dean. *Now Is Your Time! The African-American Struggle for Freedom.* New York: HarperCollins, 1992. An overview of African-American history from slavery to the present. (Ages 10-up)

Parks, Rosa. *Rosa Parks: Mother to a Movement.* New York: Dial, 1992. An autobiography of the woman whose protest led to the Montgomery bus boycott. (Ages 11-up)

Plowden, Martha Ward. *Famous Firsts of Black Women.* Gretna, LA: Pelican Publishing Co., 1993. Includes famous African-American women from the worlds of sports, business, and the arts. (Ages 10-up)

Stein, Richard C. *The Montgomery Bus Boycott.* Chicago: Children's Press, 1993. A detailed discussion of the Montgomery bus boycott and the people who made it a success. (Ages 7–12)

Wilkinson, Brenda. *Jesse Jackson: Still Fighting for the Dream.* Englewood Cliffs, NJ: Silver Burdett Press, 1990. Biography of civil rights activist and politician who marched with Dr. King and continues to strive toward equal rights for all Americans. (Ages 10-up)

BIBLIOGRAPHY

Ebony Magazine. *Ebony Pictorial History of Black America.* 3 vols. Nashville, TN: The Southwestern Company, 1971.

Time-Life Books. *African American Voices of Triumph: Perseverance.* Foreword by Henry Louis Gates, Jr., Alexandria, Va: Time-Life Custom Publishing, 1993.

"Lorraine Motel Opens Its Doors Again." *Tennessee Teacher.* January 1992: 9–15.

Low, W. Augustus, and Virgil A. Clift, eds. "Civil Rights." In *Encyclopedia of Black America.* New York: Da Capo Press, 1984.

McKissack, Patricia, and Fred McKissack. *The Civil Rights Movement in America: From 1865 to the Present.* 2nd ed. Chicago: Children's Press, 1991.

Miller, Marilyn. *The Bridge at Selma.* Morristown, NJ: Silver Burdett Press, 1984.

Ploski, Harry A. and James Williams, eds. "Chronology: A Historical Review." In *The Negro Almanac: A Reference Work on the Afro-American.* New York: John Wiley & Sons, 1983.

Thomas, Keith. "Keeping the Dream." *Atlanta Constitution,* 30 June 1991, Section M, 1–6.

Thomas, William. "Building a Dream: Death of Dr. King Created an Indelible Mark Here." *Commercial Appeal,* Memphis, TN, 30 June 1991, Section G, 1–9.

Washington, James M., ed. *A Testament of Hope: The Essential Speeches and Writings of Martin Luther King, Jr.* New York: Harper & Row, 1986.

INDEX

ACKNOWLEDGMENTS

My part in this book is due to many positive forces. I should first thank my mother and father, Earline and Kenneth Duncan, who made it all possible. Many thanks go to librarian Lois Collins for the use of her library collection. And for all of their support and encouragement, I want to thank my "core" group: Shun, Karen, Jeff, and Tim. To the other major players who turned this vision into a reality, I say thanks to Leila Boyd for the morale boost and paper, while much gratitude goes to Jim Smith, Bonnie Brook, Leslie Bauman, and BridgeWater Books for choosing me.

Alice Faye Duncan

I am thankful to many people who helped me with this book—my wife, Anne, who started me on the journey that led to the National Civil Rights Museum, and four wonderful women: Juanita Moore, Leila Boyd, Barbara Andrews, and Rosalyn Nichols, all of whom opened the museum and their hearts to me.

I want to thank my own children, Laura, Luke, and Alison, who were a source of encouragement and humor; and all the children pictured in this book—they were so eager to help!

A special debt of gratitude goes to Matt and Andrew Gillis, Leslie Bauman, Beaura Ringrose, Bonnie Brook, and Alice Faye Duncan, with one final thanks to all the men, women, and children who marched on the journey for civil rights. Their struggle leaves me moved, inspired, and finally humbled.

J. Gerard Smith

CREDITS

Every effort has been made to secure the necessary permissions and make full acknowledgment for their use. If notified of any errors, the publisher will gladly make the necessary corrections in future editions.

Text Credits Excerpts from "Letter from a Birmingham Jail," "I Have a Dream," and "I've Seen the Promised Land," by Dr. Martin Luther King, Jr., reprinted by arrangement with The Heirs to the Estate of Martin Luther King, Jr., c/o Joan Daves Agency as agent for the proprietor. Copyright © 1963 by Martin Luther King, Jr.; copyright renewed 1991 by Coretta Scott King ("Letter from a Birmingham Jail" and "I Have a Dream"). Copyright © 1968 by the Estate of Martin Luther King, Jr. ("I've Seen the Promised Land").

Photo Credits A/P Wide World Photos: 16 (bottom), 20, 21 (right), 24 (photographed by Fred Blackwell), 26 (right), 30 (left), 35, 38, 51; Birmingham News Company: 26 (left); Black Star: 30 (right, photographed by Charles Moore); Life Magazine, Time Warner: 56 (Joseph Law); The National Civil Rights Museum: 16 (top, photographed by Don Craven); UPI/Bettman: 21 (left), 27, 32, 34, 36, 41, 42, 43, 45, 46.